Alfred's Basic Piano Library

Prep Course

FOR THE YOUNG BEGINNER

Sacred Solos • Level D

Willard A. Palmer • Morton Manus • Amanda Vick Lethco

This book may be begun when the student has learned *AMIGOS,* on page 13 in PREP LESSON BOOK D of Alfred's Basic Piano Library.

The music is coordinated with Prep Lesson Book D, and assignments may be made in accordance with the instructions in the upper right corner of the first page of each hymn.

Many students are especially interested in learning to play sacred music, and many parents are very pleased when their children can play a repertoire of familiar hymns. Because of this, the pieces in this book provide motivation of a kind offered by almost no other type of music, and, as these pieces are mastered, they provide valuable opportunities for reinforcement of many of the principles that are emphasized in Lesson Book D.

Sacred music is always appropriate for private performances for family and friends, as well as for public performances at recitals, clubs, social gatherings, and church functions.

DUETS: Each hymn in this book has a duet part that may be played on the same piano, together with the solo part. These hymns make excellent student-teacher or student-parent duets, or they may be played by two students of varying levels of advancement. The solo and duet parts contain measure numbers for easy reference during rehearsal. The student parts are complete as solos without the addition of the duet part.

Illustrations by Christine Finn

Use after AMIGOS (page 13).

The first part of this piece is played with both hands in C POSITION.
On the next page the RH moves to G POSITION; LH remains in C POSITION.
For the last two lines, the RH returns to C POSITION.

Jesus, Lover of My Soul

Words by Charles Wesley
Music by Simeon B. Marsh

Moderately

1. Je - sus, Lov - er of my soul, Let me
2. While the near - er wa - ters roll, While the

to Thy bos - om is fly.
tem - pest still fly. high.

2nd time move RH to G POSITION.

DUET PART: (Student plays 1 octave higher.)

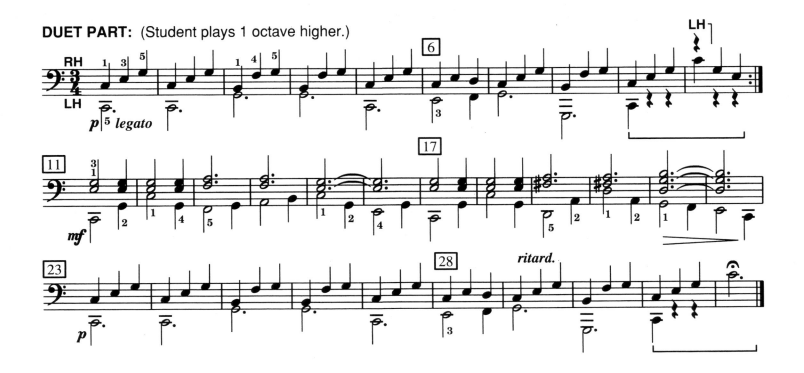

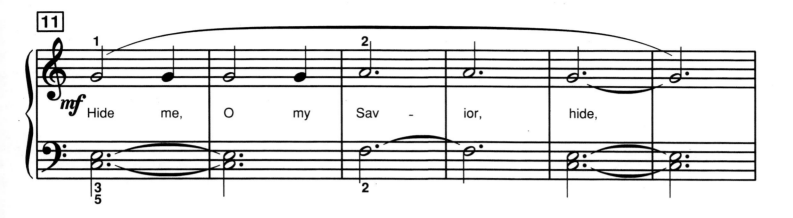

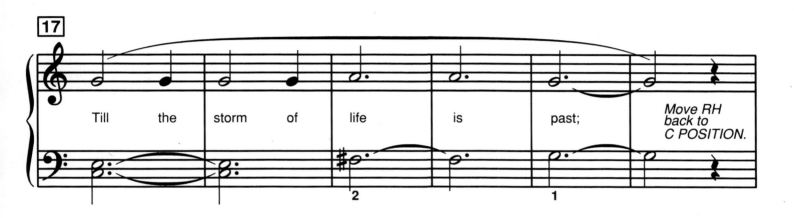

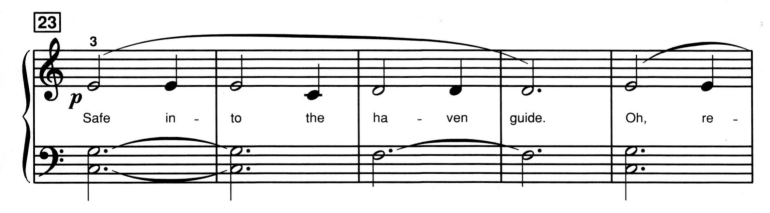

Use after MY COMPUTER (pages 14–15).

Johannes Crüger (1598–1663) was one of the greatest composers of sacred chorales. One of his best known is used for two communion hymns, this one and "Feed Thy Children, God Most Holy," the words of which are given at the bottom of the next page.

Soul, Adorn Thyself with Gladness

C POSITION

Words by Johann Franck
Music by Johannes Crüger

Happily, but not too fast!

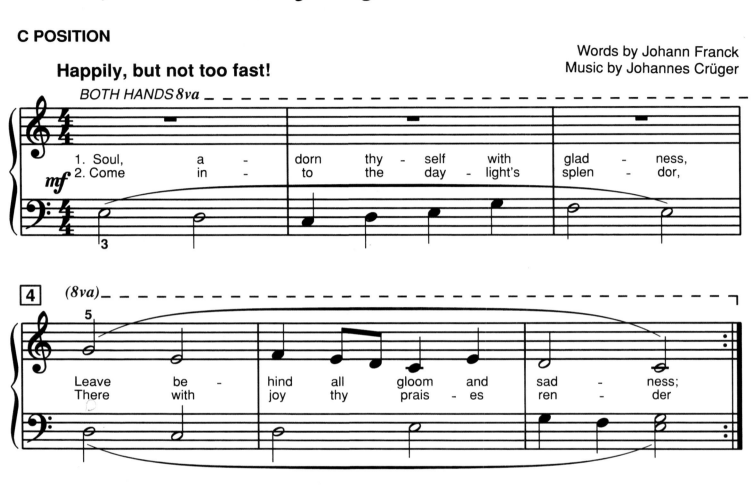

Lyrics under staff:
1. Soul, a - dorn thy - self with glad - ness,
2. Come in - to the day - light's splen - dor,

Leave be - hind all gloom and sad - ness;
There with joy thy prais - es ren - der

DUET PART: (Student plays ENTIRE solo part 8va, including the measures not so marked.)

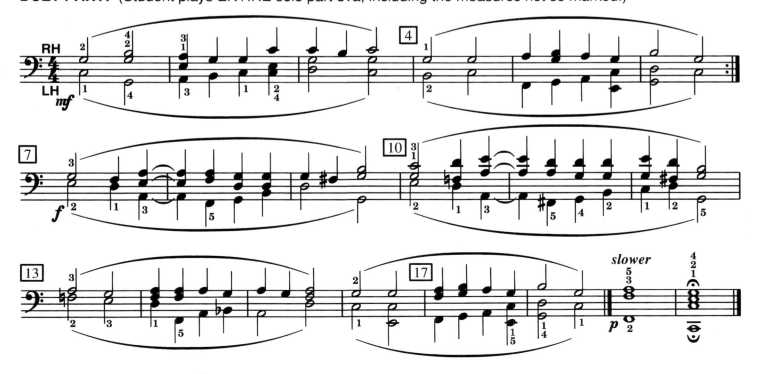

FEED THY CHILDREN, GOD MOST HOLY
(Words by Johann Heermann)

Feed Thy children, God most holy,
Comfort sinners poor and lowly;
O Thou Bread of Life from heaven,
Bless the food Thou here hast given!
As these gifts the body nourish,
May our souls in graces flourish
Till with saints in heav'nly splendor
At Thy feast due thanks we render. Amen.

Use after MINUET AND TRIO (pages 16–17).

The Great Physician Now Is Near

Words by William Hunter
Music by John H. Stockton

Andante moderato

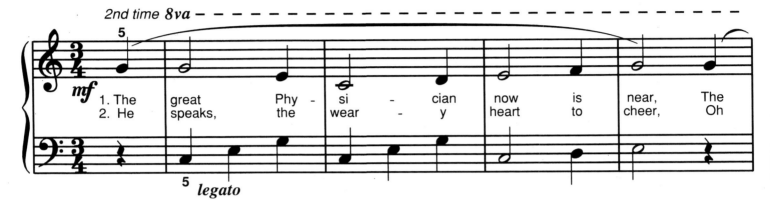

After 2nd time move
RH to G POSITION

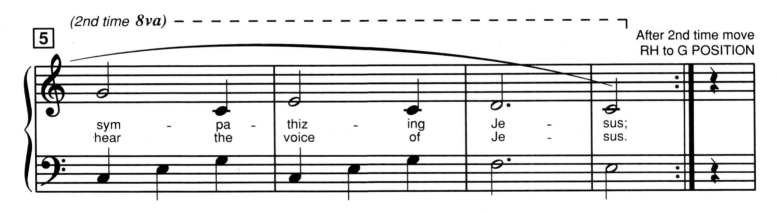

DUET PART: (Student plays BOTH HANDS 8va throughout!)

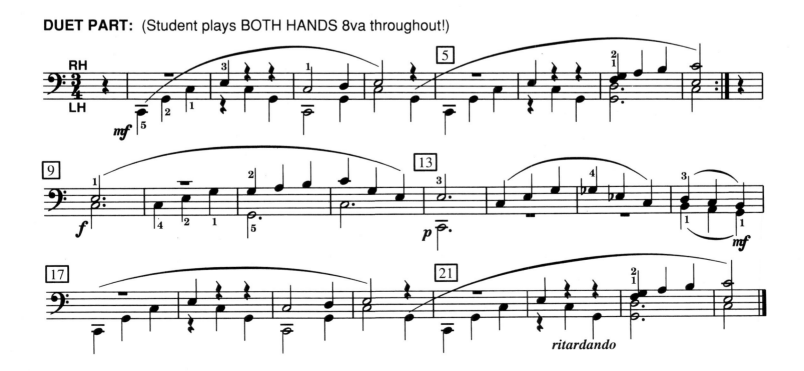

2. Your many sins are all forgiv'n,
   Oh hear the voice of Jesus;
   Go on your way in peace to heav'n,
   And wear the crown of Jesus!
   CHORUS

3. His name dispels my doubt and fear,
   No other name but Jesus,
   Oh how my soul delights to hear
   The lovely name of Jesus!
   CHORUS

Sun of My Soul

RH in D POSITION
LH in HIGH G POSITION

Use after FOUR POSITION MARCH (page 18).

Words by John Keble
Music by Peter Ritter

Moderato

Sun of my soul! Thou Sav - ior dear,

DUET PART: (Student plays 1 octave higher.)

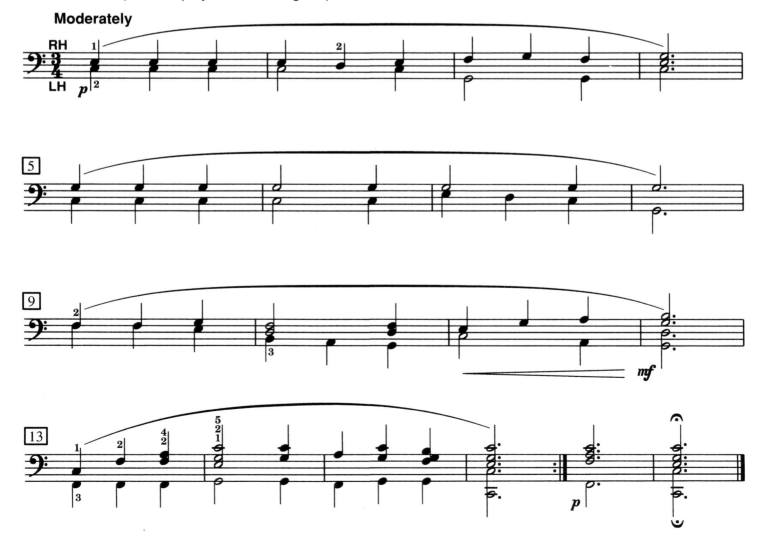

Moderately

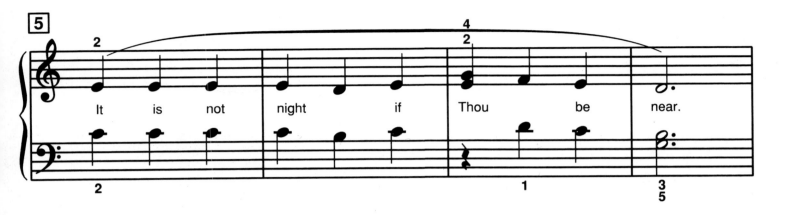

It is not night if Thou be near.

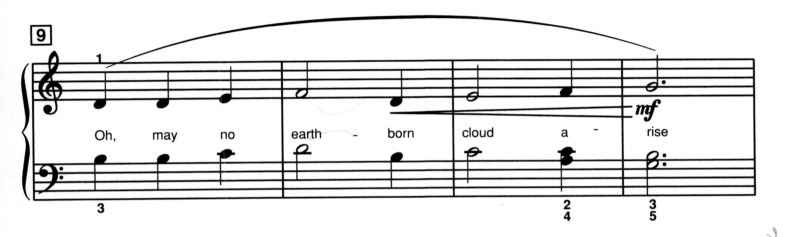

Oh, may no earth - born cloud a - rise *mf*

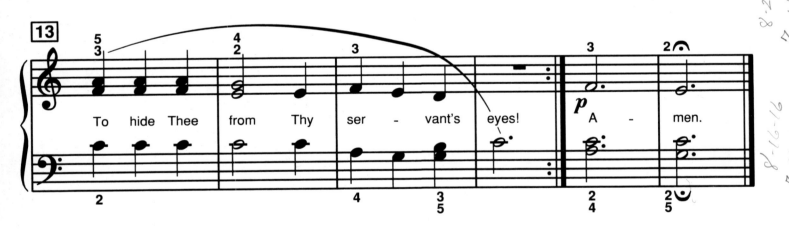

To hide Thee from Thy ser - vant's eyes! *p* A - men.

2. When the soft dews of kindly sleep
My weary eyelids gently steep,
Be my last thought, how sweet to rest
Forever on my Savior's breast!

3. Abide with me from morn till eve,
For without Thee I cannot live.
Abide with me when night is nigh,
For without Thee I dare not die.

4. Be near and bless me when I wake,
Ere through the world my way I take,
Abide with me till in Thy love
I lose myself in heav'n above.

Tell Me the Story of Jesus

Use after HARP SONG (page 23).

Words by Fanny J. Crosby
Music by Willard A. Palmer

Moderato

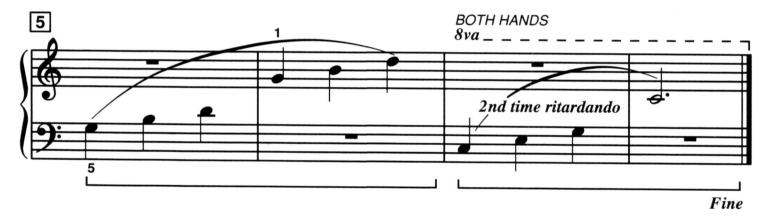

DUET PART: (Student plays 1 octave higher.)

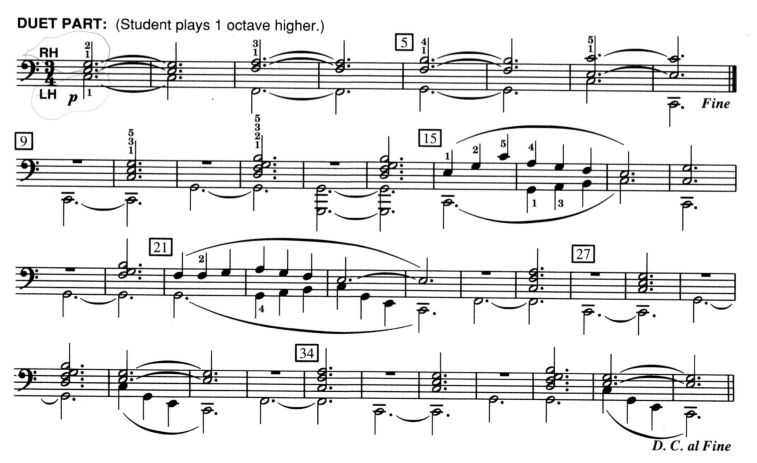

D. C. al Fine

D. C. al Fine

Use after THE PLANETS (page 31).

God Made Them All!

MIDDLE C WHOLE-STEP POSITION

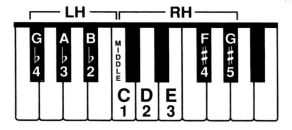

(RH C & D are not used in this piece.)

Adagio moderato

Willard A. Palmer

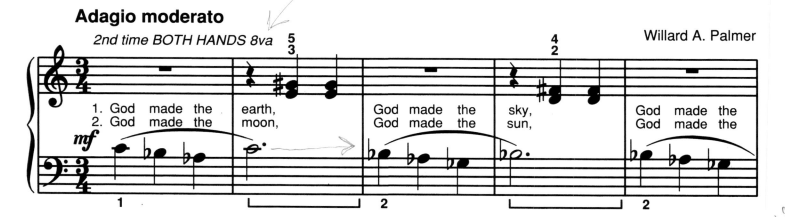

1. God made the earth,   God made the sky,   God made the
2. God made the moon,   God made the sun,   God made the

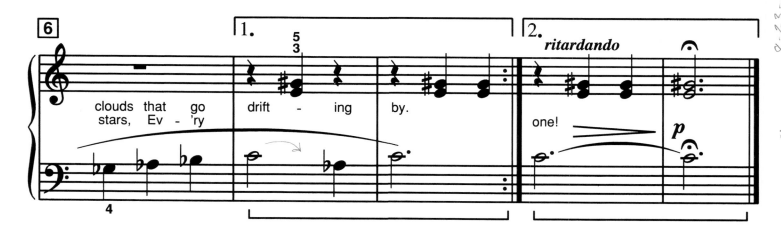

clouds that go   drift - ing   by.   one!
stars, Ev - 'ry

ritardando

DUET PART: Play this part 1 octave higher 1st time;
2 octaves higher 2nd time.

ritardando

Thine Forever! God of Love

USING C & G TETRACHORDS

HAND POSITION:

LH plays the lower (C) tetrachord.
RH plays the upper (G) tetrachord.

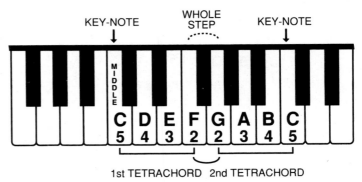

Moderato

Words & Music by Mary Fowler Maude

1. Thine for - ev - er! God of love. Hear us
2. Thine for - ev - er! O how blest They who

from Thy throne a - bove; Thine for - ev - er may we
find in Thee their rest! Sav - ior, Guard - ian, heav'n - ly

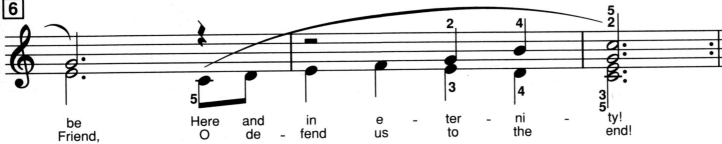

be Here and in e - ter - ni - ty!
Friend, O de - fend us to the end!

DUET PART

Use after THE MERMAID (pages 40–41).

I Surrender All

USING G & D TETRACHORDS

HAND POSITION:

RH plays the upper (D) tetrachord,
LH plays the lower (G) tetrachord.

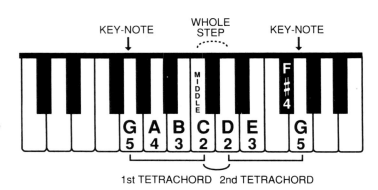

IMPORTANT! Before playing this piece, clap (or tap) and count the following rhythm*:

COUNT: "one & two & three & four &, one & two & three & four &"

KEY OF G MAJOR
Key Signature: 1 sharp (F♯)
Play all "F's" sharp throughout.

Words by J. W. Van Deventer
Melody by W. S. Weeden

Moderato

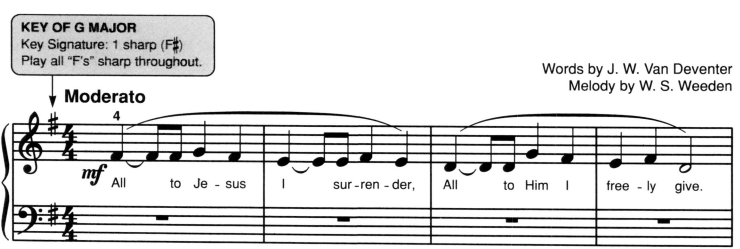

All to Je - sus I sur -ren - der, All to Him I free - ly give.

DUET PART: (Student plays 1 octave higher.)

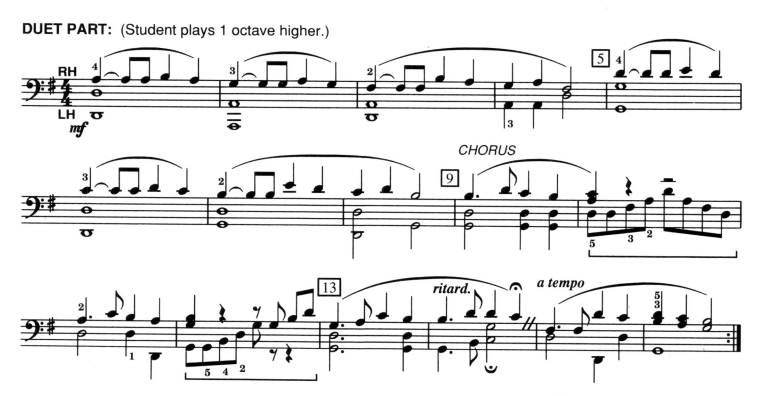

*This is a simple preparation for the dotted quarter & eighth note rhythm, which will be introduced
in Prep Level E or in the Level 2 Lesson Book.

5 I will ev - er love and trust Him, in His pres - ence dai - ly live.

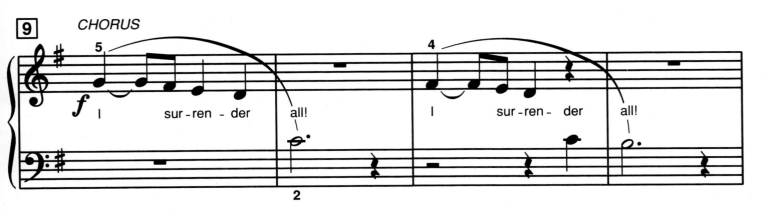

9 *CHORUS*

f I sur - ren - der all! I sur - ren - der all!

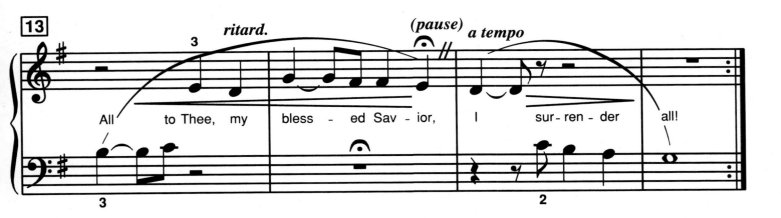

13 *ritard.* *(pause)* *a tempo*

All to Thee, my bless - ed Sav - ior, I sur - ren - der all!

2. All to Jesus I surrender,
   Humbly at His feet I bow,
   Worldly pleasures all forsaken,
   Take me, Jesus, take me now.
   CHORUS

3. All to Jesus I surrender,
   Make me, Savior, wholly Thine;
   May Thy Holy Spirit fill me,
   May I know Thy pow'r divine.
   CHORUS

4. All to Jesus I surrender,
   Lord, I give myself to Thee;
   Fill me with Thy love and power,
   Let Thy blessing fall on me.
   CHORUS

Use after THE BASEBALL GAME (pages 44–45).

This Little Light Is Gonna Shine

RH in C POSITION
LH in LOW G POSITION

Happily

Spiritual

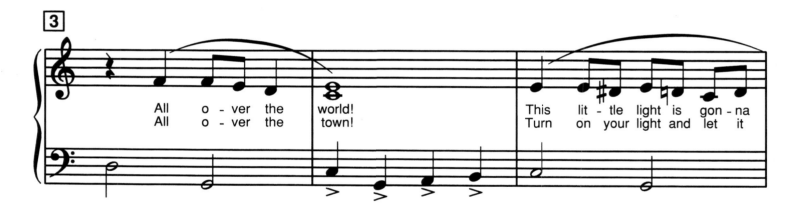

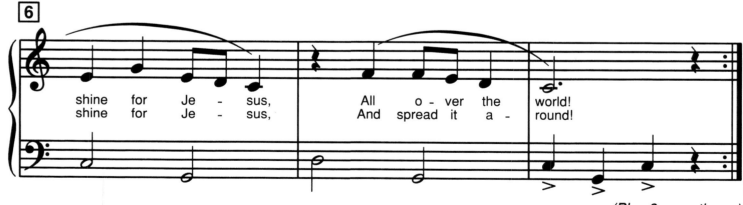

(Play 2 more times.)

DUET PART: (Student plays both hands 8va throughout.)